SELF care

self care journal

FOR A LITTLE INSPIRATION
follow along at:

@JUNEANDLUCY

@JUNEANDLUCY

WWW.JUNELUCY.COM

Love free goodies? Join our newsletter by emailing us at **freebies@junelucy.com** to receive freebies, discounts and sales info. Let us know which book you bought by putting the book title in the subject line of your email.

Shop our other books at www.junelucy.com

For questions and customer service, email us at support@junelucy.com

This Journal Belongs to:

Your Self-Care Journal

In today's world, it can seem like our "to-do list" remains a mile long while we are pulled in dozens of different directions. Work life, family life, friendships, and housework add up to more than a full-time job which leaves us with the question: where is the time for a little self-care? Remember, you can't pour from an empty cup! Making time for a little self-care each day results in tons of benefits: better sleep, less stress, a more positive outlook, and a better overall quality of life. "Self-care" doesn't have to mean a luxurious trip to the spa or reservations at a five-star restaurant (although it is fun to splurge on yourself once in a while). It can be as simple as a phone call with a friend, an evening bubble bath, or a few minutes of journaling.

This journal presents daily pages that set you up to integrate self-care into your everyday routine without having to overthink it. You will start the day with morning gratitude by writing down three things you are grateful for. Gratitude journaling has so many wonderful benefits and is a great building block of self-care. Your gratitude list can be as small as getting a perfectly ripe avocado or a wave from your friendly neighbor. It is important to appreciate the little things.

Next, you will document how you slept the night before. Sleep is so important to your physical health, cognitive function, and overall mood. A commitment to getting better sleep is a commitment to yourself. Keeping track of your sleep habits will help cultivate better patterns and better sleep overall.

Each daily journal page also includes space to document how you nourished your body by writing down some healthy things you ate and some things you treated yourself with. And remember: the treats don't have to be chips or sweets (although they can be!). On a hot summer day, the best treat may be an ice-cold glass of water or bowl of fresh fruit. Also be sure to document your water intake and circle any physical activity you have completed that day (exercises, stretching, meditation).

Next, write down one thing your body thanked you for today. Here is where you can document that new workout you tried, the walk in the park you took, or the new recipe you made for dinner. Our mental and emotional health is inextricably linked to our physical health, so try to do at least one thing per day that will make your body say, "Thanks, friend!"

Finally, complete a little evening wind-down by jotting down three things you're doing to promote a peaceful night. These can be things like drinking a warm mug of chamomile tea with honey, reading a chapter of your favorite book, or lighting a delicious smelling candle while you do your skincare routine. Nighttime rituals help prepare our body and mind for a restful and restorative sleep.

On each daily layout, you will also find your "Self-Care Checklist" page. This is a list of suggestions to incorporate into your daily life. Try to check off at least one of these items per day. And remember, self-care doesn't have to be time-intensive or expensive. Many of these items can be completed in five minutes.

Sprinkled throughout this journal, you will also find encouraging quotes and extra self-care exercises. So please remember: self-care is not selfish!

DATE: ____________________ S M T W T F S

morning gratitude

1. ____________________
2. ____________________
3. ____________________

a little beauty sleep

SLEEP DURATION — SLEPT FROM ______ to ______ TOTAL SLEEP TIME ______ hrs ______ min

SLEEP QUALITY — ☐ SOUND ☐ RESTLESS ☐ FREQUENT INTERRUPTIONS

WHAT WOKE ME — ☐ ALARM ☐ NATURALLY ☐ NOISE

HOW I FELT UPON WAKING — ☐ ENERGIZED ☐ REFRESHED ☐ TIRED ☐ GROGGY

an apple a day

NOURISHED MY BODY WITH ____________________

TREATED MY BODY WITH ____________________

DON'T FORGET TO *hydrate*

exercise | stretching | meditation

TODAY MY BODY THANKED ME FOR ____________________

____

____

evening wind-down

3 THINGS I'M DOING TO PROMOTE A PEACEFUL NIGHT

1. ____________________
2. ____________________
3. ____________________

SELF-CARE checklist

- ◯ bubble bath
- ◯ meditate
- ◯ read a good book
- ◯ journal
- ◯ exercise
- ◯ coffee / tea
- ◯ yoga
- ◯ be creative
- ◯ dance party
- ◯ sweet treat
- ◯ face mask
- ◯ fun purchase
- ◯ nails / beauty
- ◯ deep breathing
- ◯ time with a pet
- ◯ gratitude list
- ◯ nap / rest
- ◯ call a friend
- ◯ spend time outside
- ◯ watch something good
- ◯ game / puzzle
- ◯ new restaurant
- ◯ light a candle
- ◯ listen to music
- ◯ organize / clean
- ◯ unplug
- ◯ make a fun plan
- ◯ affirmations
- ◯ complete to-do list
- ◯ do a kind act
- ◯ hot shower
- ◯ moment of pure peace

Self-care is giving the best of you, not what's left of you.

DATE: ______________ S M T W T F S

morning gratitude

1. ______________
2. ______________
3. ______________

a little beauty sleep

SLEEP DURATION SLEPT FROM ______ to ______ TOTAL SLEEP TIME ______ hrs ______ min

SLEEP QUALITY ☐ SOUND ☐ RESTLESS ☐ FREQUENT INTERRUPTIONS

WHAT WOKE ME ☐ ALARM ☐ NATURALLY ☐ NOISE

HOW I FELT UPON WAKING ☐ ENERGIZED ☐ REFRESHED ☐ TIRED ☐ GROGGY

an apple a day

NOURISHED MY BODY WITH ______________

TREATED MY BODY WITH ______________

DON'T FORGET TO *hydrate* ☐ ☐ ☐ ☐ ☐ ☐ ☐ ☐

exercise | stretching | meditation

TODAY MY BODY THANKED ME FOR ______________

____

____

evening wind-down

3 THINGS I'M DOING TO PROMOTE A PEACEFUL NIGHT

1. ______________
2. ______________
3. ______________

SELF-CARE checklist

- bubble bath
- meditate
- read a good book
- journal
- exercise
- coffee / tea
- yoga
- be creative
- dance party
- sweet treat
- face mask
- fun purchase
- nails / beauty
- deep breathing
- time with a pet
- gratitude list
- nap / rest
- call a friend
- spend time outside
- watch something good
- game / puzzle
- new restaurant
- light a candle
- listen to music
- organize / clean
- unplug
- make a fun plan
- affirmations
- complete to-do list
- do a kind act
- hot shower
- moment of pure peace

Self-care is giving the best of you,
not what's left of you.

DATE: ______________________ S M T W T F S

morning gratitude

1. ______________________
2. ______________________
3. ______________________

a little beauty sleep

SLEEP DURATION — SLEPT FROM ________ to ________ TOTAL SLEEP TIME ________ hrs ________ min

SLEEP QUALITY — ☐ SOUND ☐ RESTLESS ☐ FREQUENT INTERRUPTIONS

WHAT WOKE ME — ☐ ALARM ☐ NATURALLY ☐ NOISE

HOW I FELT UPON WAKING — ☐ ENERGIZED ☐ REFRESHED ☐ TIRED ☐ GROGGY

an apple a day

NOURISHED MY BODY WITH ______________________

TREATED MY BODY WITH ______________________

DON'T FORGET TO *hydrate* ☐ ☐ ☐ ☐ ☐ ☐ ☐ ☐

exercise | stretching | meditation

TODAY MY BODY THANKED ME FOR ______________________

____

____

evening wind-down

3 THINGS I'M DOING TO PROMOTE A PEACEFUL NIGHT

1. ______________________
2. ______________________
3. ______________________

SELF-CARE checklist

- ○ bubble bath
- ○ meditate
- ○ read a good book
- ○ journal
- ○ exercise
- ○ coffee / tea
- ○ yoga
- ○ be creative
- ○ dance party
- ○ sweet treat
- ○ face mask
- ○ fun purchase
- ○ nails / beauty
- ○ deep breathing
- ○ time with a pet
- ○ gratitude list
- ○ nap / rest
- ○ call a friend
- ○ spend time outside
- ○ watch something good
- ○ game / puzzle
- ○ new restaurant
- ○ light a candle
- ○ listen to music
- ○ organize / clean
- ○ unplug
- ○ make a fun plan
- ○ affirmations
- ○ complete to-do list
- ○ do a kind act
- ○ hot shower
- ○ moment of pure peace

Self-care is giving the best of you,
not what's left of you.

DATE: ____________________ S M T W T F S

morning gratitude

1. ____________________
2. ____________________
3. ____________________

a little beauty sleep

SLEEP DURATION — SLEPT FROM ________ to ________ TOTAL SLEEP TIME ________ hrs ________ min

SLEEP QUALITY — ☐ SOUND ☐ RESTLESS ☐ FREQUENT INTERRUPTIONS

WHAT WOKE ME — ☐ ALARM ☐ NATURALLY ☐ NOISE

HOW I FELT UPON WAKING — ☐ ENERGIZED ☐ REFRESHED ☐ TIRED ☐ GROGGY

an apple a day

NOURISHED MY BODY WITH ____________________

TREATED MY BODY WITH ____________________

DON'T FORGET TO *hydrate* ☐ ☐ ☐ ☐ ☐ ☐ ☐ ☐

exercise | stretching | meditation

TODAY MY BODY THANKED ME FOR ____________________

____

____

evening wind-down

3 THINGS I'M DOING TO PROMOTE A PEACEFUL NIGHT

1. ____________________
2. ____________________
3. ____________________

SELF-CARE
checklist

- ◯ bubble bath
- ◯ meditate
- ◯ read a good book
- ◯ journal
- ◯ exercise
- ◯ coffee / tea
- ◯ yoga
- ◯ be creative
- ◯ dance party
- ◯ sweet treat
- ◯ face mask
- ◯ fun purchase
- ◯ nails / beauty
- ◯ deep breathing
- ◯ time with a pet
- ◯ gratitude list
- ◯ nap / rest
- ◯ call a friend
- ◯ spend time outside
- ◯ watch something good
- ◯ game / puzzle
- ◯ new restaurant
- ◯ light a candle
- ◯ listen to music
- ◯ organize / clean
- ◯ unplug
- ◯ make a fun plan
- ◯ affirmations
- ◯ complete to-do list
- ◯ do a kind act
- ◯ hot shower
- ◯ moment of pure peace

Self-care is giving the best of you,
not what's left of you.

DATE: ______________________ S M T W T F S

morning gratitude

1. ______________________

2. ______________________

3. ______________________

a little beauty sleep

SLEEP DURATION — SLEPT FROM ________ to ________ TOTAL SLEEP TIME ________ hrs ________ min

SLEEP QUALITY — ☐ SOUND ☐ RESTLESS ☐ FREQUENT INTERRUPTIONS

WHAT WOKE ME — ☐ ALARM ☐ NATURALLY ☐ NOISE

HOW I FELT UPON WAKING — ☐ ENERGIZED ☐ REFRESHED ☐ TIRED ☐ GROGGY

an apple a day

NOURISHED MY BODY WITH ______________________

TREATED MY BODY WITH ______________________

DON'T FORGET TO *hydrate*

exercise | stretching | meditation

TODAY MY BODY THANKED ME FOR ______________________

____

____

evening wind-down

3 THINGS I'M DOING TO PROMOTE A PEACEFUL NIGHT

1. ______________________

2. ______________________

3. ______________________

SELF-CARE
checklist

- ○ bubble bath
- ○ meditate
- ○ read a good book
- ○ journal
- ○ exercise
- ○ coffee / tea
- ○ yoga
- ○ be creative
- ○ dance party
- ○ sweet treat
- ○ face mask
- ○ fun purchase
- ○ nails / beauty
- ○ deep breathing
- ○ time with a pet
- ○ gratitude list
- ○ nap / rest
- ○ call a friend
- ○ spend time outside
- ○ watch something good
- ○ game / puzzle
- ○ new restaurant
- ○ light a candle
- ○ listen to music
- ○ organize / clean
- ○ unplug
- ○ make a fun plan
- ○ affirmations
- ○ complete to-do list
- ○ do a kind act
- ○ hot shower
- ○ moment of pure peace

Self-care is giving the best of you,
not what's left of you.

It's not selfish,
it's self-care

A little extra self-care

Detail below your perfect self-care evening and then schedule a night to implement it soon. Maybe you set up an at-home spa with a scented bubble bath, candles, and face masks. Or turn your living room into a movie theater with comfy cushions and all the snacks.

DATE: ______________________ S M T W T F S

morning gratitude

1. ______________________

2. ______________________

3. ______________________

a little beauty sleep

SLEEP DURATION — SLEPT FROM ________ to ________ TOTAL SLEEP TIME ________ hrs ________ min

SLEEP QUALITY — ☐ SOUND ☐ RESTLESS ☐ FREQUENT INTERRUPTIONS

WHAT WOKE ME — ☐ ALARM ☐ NATURALLY ☐ NOISE

HOW I FELT UPON WAKING — ☐ ENERGIZED ☐ REFRESHED ☐ TIRED ☐ GROGGY

an apple a day

NOURISHED MY BODY WITH ______________________

TREATED MY BODY WITH ______________________

DON'T FORGET TO *hydrate* ☐ ☐ ☐ ☐ ☐ ☐ ☐ ☐

exercise | stretching | meditation

TODAY MY BODY THANKED ME FOR ______________________

____

____

evening wind-down

3 THINGS I'M DOING TO PROMOTE A PEACEFUL NIGHT

1. ______________________

2. ______________________

3. ______________________

SELF-CARE checklist

- bubble bath
- meditate
- read a good book
- journal
- exercise
- coffee / tea
- yoga
- be creative
- dance party
- sweet treat
- face mask
- fun purchase
- nails / beauty
- deep breathing
- time with a pet
- gratitude list
- nap / rest
- call a friend
- spend time outside
- watch something good
- game / puzzle
- new restaurant
- light a candle
- listen to music
- organize / clean
- unplug
- make a fun plan
- affirmations
- complete to-do list
- do a kind act
- hot shower
- moment of pure peace

Self-care is giving the best of you,
not what's left of you.

DATE: ______________________ S M T W T F S

morning gratitude

1. ______________________
2. ______________________
3. ______________________

a little beauty sleep

SLEEP DURATION SLEPT FROM ______ to ______ TOTAL SLEEP TIME ______ hrs ______ min

SLEEP QUALITY ☐ SOUND ☐ RESTLESS ☐ FREQUENT INTERRUPTIONS

WHAT WOKE ME ☐ ALARM ☐ NATURALLY ☐ NOISE

HOW I FELT UPON WAKING ☐ ENERGIZED ☐ REFRESHED ☐ TIRED ☐ GROGGY

an apple a day

NOURISHED MY BODY WITH ______________________

TREATED MY BODY WITH ______________________

DON'T FORGET TO *hydrate* ☐ ☐ ☐ ☐ ☐ ☐ ☐ ☐

exercise | stretching | meditation

TODAY MY BODY THANKED ME FOR ______________________

____

____

evening wind-down

3 THINGS I'M DOING TO PROMOTE A PEACEFUL NIGHT

1. ______________________
2. ______________________
3. ______________________

SELF-CARE checklist

- bubble bath
- meditate
- read a good book
- journal
- exercise
- coffee / tea
- yoga
- be creative
- dance party
- sweet treat
- face mask
- fun purchase
- nails / beauty
- deep breathing
- time with a pet
- gratitude list
- nap / rest
- call a friend
- spend time outside
- watch something good
- game / puzzle
- new restaurant
- light a candle
- listen to music
- organize / clean
- unplug
- make a fun plan
- affirmations
- complete to-do list
- do a kind act
- hot shower
- moment of pure peace

Self-care is giving the best of you,
not what's left of you.

DATE: ______________________ S M T W T F S

morning gratitude

1. ______________________

2. ______________________

3. ______________________

a little beauty sleep

SLEEP DURATION — SLEPT FROM ________ to ________ TOTAL SLEEP TIME ________ hrs ________ min

SLEEP QUALITY — ☐ SOUND ☐ RESTLESS ☐ FREQUENT INTERRUPTIONS

WHAT WOKE ME — ☐ ALARM ☐ NATURALLY ☐ NOISE

HOW I FELT UPON WAKING — ☐ ENERGIZED ☐ REFRESHED ☐ TIRED ☐ GROGGY

an apple a day

NOURISHED MY BODY WITH ______________________

TREATED MY BODY WITH ______________________

DON'T FORGET TO *hydrate* ☐ ☐ ☐ ☐ ☐ ☐ ☐ ☐

exercise | stretching | meditation

TODAY MY BODY THANKED ME FOR ______________________

____

____

evening wind-down

3 THINGS I'M DOING TO PROMOTE A PEACEFUL NIGHT

1. ______________________

2. ______________________

3. ______________________

SELF-CARE checklist

- ○ bubble bath
- ○ meditate
- ○ read a good book
- ○ journal
- ○ exercise
- ○ coffee / tea
- ○ yoga
- ○ be creative
- ○ dance party
- ○ sweet treat
- ○ face mask
- ○ fun purchase
- ○ nails / beauty
- ○ deep breathing
- ○ time with a pet
- ○ gratitude list
- ○ nap / rest
- ○ call a friend
- ○ spend time outside
- ○ watch something good
- ○ game / puzzle
- ○ new restaurant
- ○ light a candle
- ○ listen to music
- ○ organize / clean
- ○ unplug
- ○ make a fun plan
- ○ affirmations
- ○ complete to-do list
- ○ do a kind act
- ○ hot shower
- ○ moment of pure peace

Self-care is giving the best of you,
not what's left of you.

DATE: ______________________ S M T W T F S

morning gratitude

1. ______________________

2. ______________________

3. ______________________

a little beauty sleep

SLEEP DURATION — SLEPT FROM ________ to ________ TOTAL SLEEP TIME ________ hrs ________ min

SLEEP QUALITY — ☐ SOUND ☐ RESTLESS ☐ FREQUENT INTERRUPTIONS

WHAT WOKE ME — ☐ ALARM ☐ NATURALLY ☐ NOISE

HOW I FELT UPON WAKING — ☐ ENERGIZED ☐ REFRESHED ☐ TIRED ☐ GROGGY

an apple a day

NOURISHED MY BODY WITH ______________________

TREATED MY BODY WITH ______________________

DON'T FORGET TO *hydrate* ☐ ☐ ☐ ☐ ☐ ☐ ☐ ☐

exercise | stretching | meditation

TODAY MY BODY THANKED ME FOR ______________________

____

____

evening wind-down

3 THINGS I'M DOING TO PROMOTE A PEACEFUL NIGHT

1. ______________________

2. ______________________

3. ______________________

SELF-CARE checklist

- ○ bubble bath
- ○ meditate
- ○ read a good book
- ○ journal
- ○ exercise
- ○ coffee / tea
- ○ yoga
- ○ be creative
- ○ dance party
- ○ sweet treat
- ○ face mask
- ○ fun purchase
- ○ nails / beauty
- ○ deep breathing
- ○ time with a pet
- ○ gratitude list
- ○ nap / rest
- ○ call a friend
- ○ spend time outside
- ○ watch something good
- ○ game / puzzle
- ○ new restaurant
- ○ light a candle
- ○ listen to music
- ○ organize / clean
- ○ unplug
- ○ make a fun plan
- ○ affirmations
- ○ complete to-do list
- ○ do a kind act
- ○ hot shower
- ○ moment of pure peace

Self-care is giving the best of you,
not what's left of you.

DATE: ______________________ S M T W T F S

morning gratitude

1. ______________________
2. ______________________
3. ______________________

a little beauty sleep

SLEEP DURATION — SLEPT FROM ________ to ________ TOTAL SLEEP TIME ________ hrs ________ min

SLEEP QUALITY — ☐ SOUND ☐ RESTLESS ☐ FREQUENT INTERRUPTIONS

WHAT WOKE ME — ☐ ALARM ☐ NATURALLY ☐ NOISE

HOW I FELT UPON WAKING — ☐ ENERGIZED ☐ REFRESHED ☐ TIRED ☐ GROGGY

an apple a day

NOURISHED MY BODY WITH ______________________

TREATED MY BODY WITH ______________________

DON'T FORGET TO *hydrate* ☐ ☐ ☐ ☐ ☐ ☐ ☐ ☐

exercise | stretching | meditation

TODAY MY BODY THANKED ME FOR ______________________

____

____

evening wind-down

3 THINGS I'M DOING TO PROMOTE A PEACEFUL NIGHT

1. ______________________
2. ______________________
3. ______________________

SELF-CARE checklist

- ○ bubble bath
- ○ meditate
- ○ read a good book
- ○ journal
- ○ exercise
- ○ coffee / tea
- ○ yoga
- ○ be creative
- ○ dance party
- ○ sweet treat
- ○ face mask
- ○ fun purchase
- ○ nails / beauty
- ○ deep breathing
- ○ time with a pet
- ○ gratitude list
- ○ nap / rest
- ○ call a friend
- ○ spend time outside
- ○ watch something good
- ○ game / puzzle
- ○ new restaurant
- ○ light a candle
- ○ listen to music
- ○ organize / clean
- ○ unplug
- ○ make a fun plan
- ○ affirmations
- ○ complete to-do list
- ○ do a kind act
- ○ hot shower
- ○ moment of pure peace

*Self-care is giving the best of you,
not what's left of you.*

Be kind to yourself

A little extra self-care

Describe your perfect room or bedroom. Detail the lighting, the sitting areas, the decorations. What candle scents do you love? Would you have a cozy nook for reading or maybe a vanity area for getting ready? Think about small ways in which you can make the space around you more comforting and then aim to incorporate some of these changes into your environment.

DATE: ______________________ S M T W T F S

morning gratitude

1. ____________________
2. ____________________
3. ____________________

a little beauty sleep

SLEEP DURATION — SLEPT FROM ________ to ________ TOTAL SLEEP TIME ________ hrs ________ min

SLEEP QUALITY — ☐ SOUND ☐ RESTLESS ☐ FREQUENT INTERRUPTIONS

WHAT WOKE ME — ☐ ALARM ☐ NATURALLY ☐ NOISE

HOW I FELT UPON WAKING — ☐ ENERGIZED ☐ REFRESHED ☐ TIRED ☐ GROGGY

an apple a day

NOURISHED MY BODY WITH ____________________

TREATED MY BODY WITH ____________________

DON'T FORGET TO *hydrate* ☐ ☐ ☐ ☐ ☐ ☐ ☐ ☐

exercise | stretching | meditation

TODAY MY BODY THANKED ME FOR ____________________

evening wind-down

3 THINGS I'M DOING TO PROMOTE A PEACEFUL NIGHT

1. ____________________
2. ____________________
3. ____________________

SELF-CARE checklist

- ○ bubble bath
- ○ meditate
- ○ read a good book
- ○ journal
- ○ exercise
- ○ coffee / tea
- ○ yoga
- ○ be creative
- ○ dance party
- ○ sweet treat
- ○ face mask
- ○ fun purchase
- ○ nails / beauty
- ○ deep breathing
- ○ time with a pet
- ○ gratitude list
- ○ nap / rest
- ○ call a friend
- ○ spend time outside
- ○ watch something good
- ○ game / puzzle
- ○ new restaurant
- ○ light a candle
- ○ listen to music
- ○ organize / clean
- ○ unplug
- ○ make a fun plan
- ○ affirmations
- ○ complete to-do list
- ○ do a kind act
- ○ hot shower
- ○ moment of pure peace

Self-care is giving the best of you,
not what's left of you.

DATE: ______________ S M T W T F S

morning gratitude

1. ______________
2. ______________
3. ______________

a little beauty sleep

SLEEP DURATION — SLEPT FROM ______ to ______ TOTAL SLEEP TIME ______ hrs ______ min

SLEEP QUALITY — ☐ SOUND ☐ RESTLESS ☐ FREQUENT INTERRUPTIONS

WHAT WOKE ME — ☐ ALARM ☐ NATURALLY ☐ NOISE

HOW I FELT UPON WAKING — ☐ ENERGIZED ☐ REFRESHED ☐ TIRED ☐ GROGGY

an apple a day

NOURISHED MY BODY WITH ______________

TREATED MY BODY WITH ______________

DON'T FORGET TO *hydrate* ☐ ☐ ☐ ☐ ☐ ☐ ☐ ☐

exercise | stretching | meditation

TODAY MY BODY THANKED ME FOR ______________

____

____

evening wind-down

3 THINGS I'M DOING TO PROMOTE A PEACEFUL NIGHT

1. ______________
2. ______________
3. ______________

SELF-CARE checklist

- bubble bath
- meditate
- read a good book
- journal
- exercise
- coffee / tea
- yoga
- be creative
- dance party
- sweet treat
- face mask
- fun purchase
- nails / beauty
- deep breathing
- time with a pet
- gratitude list
- nap / rest
- call a friend
- spend time outside
- watch something good
- game / puzzle
- new restaurant
- light a candle
- listen to music
- organize / clean
- unplug
- make a fun plan
- affirmations
- complete to-do list
- do a kind act
- hot shower
- moment of pure peace

Self-care is giving the best of you,
not what's left of you.

DATE: ______________________ S M T W T F S

morning gratitude

1. ______________________

2. ______________________

3. ______________________

a little beauty sleep

SLEEP DURATION — SLEPT FROM ______ to ______ TOTAL SLEEP TIME ______ hrs ______ min

SLEEP QUALITY — ☐ SOUND ☐ RESTLESS ☐ FREQUENT INTERRUPTIONS

WHAT WOKE ME — ☐ ALARM ☐ NATURALLY ☐ NOISE

HOW I FELT UPON WAKING — ☐ ENERGIZED ☐ REFRESHED ☐ TIRED ☐ GROGGY

an apple a day

NOURISHED MY BODY WITH ______________________

TREATED MY BODY WITH ______________________

DON'T FORGET TO *hydrate* ☐ ☐ ☐ ☐ ☐ ☐ ☐ ☐

exercise | stretching | meditation

TODAY MY BODY THANKED ME FOR ______________________

____

____

evening wind-down

3 THINGS I'M DOING TO PROMOTE A PEACEFUL NIGHT

1. ______________________

2. ______________________

3. ______________________

SELF-CARE checklist

- ◯ bubble bath
- ◯ meditate
- ◯ read a good book
- ◯ journal
- ◯ exercise
- ◯ coffee / tea
- ◯ yoga
- ◯ be creative
- ◯ dance party
- ◯ sweet treat
- ◯ face mask
- ◯ fun purchase
- ◯ nails / beauty
- ◯ deep breathing
- ◯ time with a pet
- ◯ gratitude list
- ◯ nap / rest
- ◯ call a friend
- ◯ spend time outside
- ◯ watch something good
- ◯ game / puzzle
- ◯ new restaurant
- ◯ light a candle
- ◯ listen to music
- ◯ organize / clean
- ◯ unplug
- ◯ make a fun plan
- ◯ affirmations
- ◯ complete to-do list
- ◯ do a kind act
- ◯ hot shower
- ◯ moment of pure peace

Self-care is giving the best of you,
not what's left of you.

DATE: ______________________ S M T W T F S

morning gratitude

1. ______________________
2. ______________________
3. ______________________

a little beauty sleep

SLEEP DURATION SLEPT FROM ______ to ______ TOTAL SLEEP TIME ______ hrs ______ min

SLEEP QUALITY ☐ SOUND ☐ RESTLESS ☐ FREQUENT INTERRUPTIONS

WHAT WOKE ME ☐ ALARM ☐ NATURALLY ☐ NOISE

HOW I FELT UPON WAKING ☐ ENERGIZED ☐ REFRESHED ☐ TIRED ☐ GROGGY

an apple a day

NOURISHED MY BODY WITH ______________________

TREATED MY BODY WITH ______________________

DON'T FORGET TO *hydrate* ☐ ☐ ☐ ☐ ☐ ☐ ☐ ☐

exercise | stretching | meditation

TODAY MY BODY THANKED ME FOR ______________________

____

____

evening wind-down

3 THINGS I'M DOING TO PROMOTE A PEACEFUL NIGHT

1. ______________________
2. ______________________
3. ______________________

SELF-CARE
checklist

- bubble bath
- meditate
- read a good book
- journal
- exercise
- coffee / tea
- yoga
- be creative
- dance party
- sweet treat
- face mask
- fun purchase
- nails / beauty
- deep breathing
- time with a pet
- gratitude list
- nap / rest
- call a friend
- spend time outside
- watch something good
- game / puzzle
- new restaurant
- light a candle
- listen to music
- organize / clean
- unplug
- make a fun plan
- affirmations
- complete to-do list
- do a kind act
- hot shower
- moment of pure peace

Self-care is giving the best of you,
not what's left of you.

DATE: ______________________ S M T W T F S

morning gratitude

1. ______________________

2. ______________________

3. ______________________

a little beauty sleep

SLEEP DURATION — SLEPT FROM ______ to ______ TOTAL SLEEP TIME ______ hrs ______ min

SLEEP QUALITY — ☐ SOUND ☐ RESTLESS ☐ FREQUENT INTERRUPTIONS

WHAT WOKE ME — ☐ ALARM ☐ NATURALLY ☐ NOISE

HOW I FELT UPON WAKING — ☐ ENERGIZED ☐ REFRESHED ☐ TIRED ☐ GROGGY

an apple a day

NOURISHED MY BODY WITH ______________________

TREATED MY BODY WITH ______________________

DON'T FORGET TO *hydrate* ☐ ☐ ☐ ☐ ☐ ☐ ☐ ☐

exercise | stretching | meditation

TODAY MY BODY THANKED ME FOR ______________________

____

____

evening wind-down

3 THINGS I'M DOING TO PROMOTE A PEACEFUL NIGHT

1. ______________________

2. ______________________

3. ______________________

SELF-CARE
checklist

- ◯ bubble bath
- ◯ meditate
- ◯ read a good book
- ◯ journal
- ◯ exercise
- ◯ coffee / tea
- ◯ yoga
- ◯ be creative
- ◯ dance party
- ◯ sweet treat
- ◯ face mask
- ◯ fun purchase
- ◯ nails / beauty
- ◯ deep breathing
- ◯ time with a pet
- ◯ gratitude list
- ◯ nap / rest
- ◯ call a friend
- ◯ spend time outside
- ◯ watch something good
- ◯ game / puzzle
- ◯ new restaurant
- ◯ light a candle
- ◯ listen to music
- ◯ organize / clean
- ◯ unplug
- ◯ make a fun plan
- ◯ affirmations
- ◯ complete to-do list
- ◯ do a kind act
- ◯ hot shower
- ◯ moment of pure peace

Self-care is giving the best of you, not what's left of you.

Work on you, for you

A little extra self-care

Make a list of ten self-care activities that appeal to you and try to check three off the list in the next week.

DATE: ______________________ S M T W T F S

morning gratitude

1. ______________________
2. ______________________
3. ______________________

a little beauty sleep

SLEEP DURATION — SLEPT FROM ________ to ________ TOTAL SLEEP TIME ________ hrs ________ min

SLEEP QUALITY — ☐ SOUND ☐ RESTLESS ☐ FREQUENT INTERRUPTIONS

WHAT WOKE ME — ☐ ALARM ☐ NATURALLY ☐ NOISE

HOW I FELT UPON WAKING — ☐ ENERGIZED ☐ REFRESHED ☐ TIRED ☐ GROGGY

an apple a day

NOURISHED MY BODY WITH ______________________

TREATED MY BODY WITH ______________________

DON'T FORGET TO *hydrate* ☐ ☐ ☐ ☐ ☐ ☐ ☐ ☐

exercise | stretching | meditation

TODAY MY BODY THANKED ME FOR ______________________

____

____

evening wind-down

3 THINGS I'M DOING TO PROMOTE A PEACEFUL NIGHT

1. ______________________
2. ______________________
3. ______________________

SELF-CARE checklist

- bubble bath
- meditate
- read a good book
- journal
- exercise
- coffee / tea
- yoga
- be creative
- dance party
- sweet treat
- face mask
- fun purchase
- nails / beauty
- deep breathing
- time with a pet
- gratitude list
- nap / rest
- call a friend
- spend time outside
- watch something good
- game / puzzle
- new restaurant
- light a candle
- listen to music
- organize / clean
- unplug
- make a fun plan
- affirmations
- complete to-do list
- do a kind act
- hot shower
- moment of pure peace

*Self-care is giving the best of you,
not what's left of you.*

DATE: ______________________ S M T W T F S

morning gratitude

1. ______________________
2. ______________________
3. ______________________

a little beauty sleep

SLEEP DURATION SLEPT FROM ________ to ________ TOTAL SLEEP TIME ________ hrs ________ min

SLEEP QUALITY ☐ SOUND ☐ RESTLESS ☐ FREQUENT INTERRUPTIONS

WHAT WOKE ME ☐ ALARM ☐ NATURALLY ☐ NOISE

HOW I FELT UPON WAKING ☐ ENERGIZED ☐ REFRESHED ☐ TIRED ☐ GROGGY

an apple a day

NOURISHED MY BODY WITH ______________________

TREATED MY BODY WITH ______________________

DON'T FORGET TO *hydrate* ☐ ☐ ☐ ☐ ☐ ☐ ☐ ☐

exercise | stretching | meditation

TODAY MY BODY THANKED ME FOR ______________________

____

____

evening wind-down

3 THINGS I'M DOING TO PROMOTE A PEACEFUL NIGHT

1. ______________________
2. ______________________
3. ______________________

SELF-CARE *checklist*

- [ ] bubble bath
- [ ] meditate
- [ ] read a good book
- [ ] journal
- [ ] exercise
- [ ] coffee / tea
- [ ] yoga
- [ ] be creative
- [ ] dance party
- [ ] sweet treat
- [ ] face mask
- [ ] fun purchase
- [ ] nails / beauty
- [ ] deep breathing
- [ ] time with a pet
- [ ] gratitude list
- [ ] nap / rest
- [ ] call a friend
- [ ] spend time outside
- [ ] watch something good
- [ ] game / puzzle
- [ ] new restaurant
- [ ] light a candle
- [ ] listen to music
- [ ] organize / clean
- [ ] unplug
- [ ] make a fun plan
- [ ] affirmations
- [ ] complete to-do list
- [ ] do a kind act
- [ ] hot shower
- [ ] moment of pure peace

Self-care is giving the best of you,
not what's left of you.

DATE: ______________________ S M T W T F S

morning gratitude

1. ______________________

2. ______________________

3. ______________________

a little beauty sleep

SLEEP DURATION — SLEPT FROM ________ to ________ TOTAL SLEEP TIME ________ hrs ________ min

SLEEP QUALITY — ☐ SOUND ☐ RESTLESS ☐ FREQUENT INTERRUPTIONS

WHAT WOKE ME — ☐ ALARM ☐ NATURALLY ☐ NOISE

HOW I FELT UPON WAKING — ☐ ENERGIZED ☐ REFRESHED ☐ TIRED ☐ GROGGY

an apple a day

NOURISHED MY BODY WITH ______________________

TREATED MY BODY WITH ______________________

DON'T FORGET TO *hydrate* ☐ ☐ ☐ ☐ ☐ ☐ ☐ ☐

exercise | stretching | meditation

TODAY MY BODY THANKED ME FOR ______________________

____

____

evening wind-down

3 THINGS I'M DOING TO PROMOTE A PEACEFUL NIGHT

1. ______________________

2. ______________________

3. ______________________

SELF-CARE checklist

- bubble bath
- meditate
- read a good book
- journal
- exercise
- coffee / tea
- yoga
- be creative
- dance party
- sweet treat
- face mask
- fun purchase
- nails / beauty
- deep breathing
- time with a pet
- gratitude list
- nap / rest
- call a friend
- spend time outside
- watch something good
- game / puzzle
- new restaurant
- light a candle
- listen to music
- organize / clean
- unplug
- make a fun plan
- affirmations
- complete to-do list
- do a kind act
- hot shower
- moment of pure peace

Self-care is giving the best of you,
not what's left of you.

DATE: ______________________ S M T W T F S

morning gratitude

1. ______________________

2. ______________________

3. ______________________

a little beauty sleep

SLEEP DURATION — SLEPT FROM ______ to ______ TOTAL SLEEP TIME ______ hrs ______ min

SLEEP QUALITY — ☐ SOUND ☐ RESTLESS ☐ FREQUENT INTERRUPTIONS

WHAT WOKE ME — ☐ ALARM ☐ NATURALLY ☐ NOISE

HOW I FELT UPON WAKING — ☐ ENERGIZED ☐ REFRESHED ☐ TIRED ☐ GROGGY

an apple a day

NOURISHED MY BODY WITH ______________________

TREATED MY BODY WITH ______________________

DON'T FORGET TO *hydrate* ☐ ☐ ☐ ☐ ☐ ☐ ☐ ☐

exercise | stretching | meditation

TODAY MY BODY THANKED ME FOR ______________________

____

____

evening wind-down

3 THINGS I'M DOING TO PROMOTE A PEACEFUL NIGHT

1. ______________________

2. ______________________

3. ______________________

SELF-CARE checklist

- ◯ bubble bath
- ◯ meditate
- ◯ read a good book
- ◯ journal
- ◯ exercise
- ◯ coffee / tea
- ◯ yoga
- ◯ be creative
- ◯ dance party
- ◯ sweet treat
- ◯ face mask
- ◯ fun purchase
- ◯ nails / beauty
- ◯ deep breathing
- ◯ time with a pet
- ◯ gratitude list
- ◯ nap / rest
- ◯ call a friend
- ◯ spend time outside
- ◯ watch something good
- ◯ game / puzzle
- ◯ new restaurant
- ◯ light a candle
- ◯ listen to music
- ◯ organize / clean
- ◯ unplug
- ◯ make a fun plan
- ◯ affirmations
- ◯ complete to-do list
- ◯ do a kind act
- ◯ hot shower
- ◯ moment of pure peace

Self-care is giving the best of you,
not what's left of you.

DATE: ____________ S M T W T F S

morning gratitude

1. ____________
2. ____________
3. ____________

a little beauty sleep

SLEEP DURATION — SLEPT FROM ______ to ______ TOTAL SLEEP TIME ______ hrs ______ min

SLEEP QUALITY — ☐ SOUND ☐ RESTLESS ☐ FREQUENT INTERRUPTIONS

WHAT WOKE ME — ☐ ALARM ☐ NATURALLY ☐ NOISE

HOW I FELT UPON WAKING — ☐ ENERGIZED ☐ REFRESHED ☐ TIRED ☐ GROGGY

an apple a day

NOURISHED MY BODY WITH ____________

TREATED MY BODY WITH ____________

DON'T FORGET TO *hydrate* ☐ ☐ ☐ ☐ ☐ ☐ ☐ ☐

exercise | stretching | meditation

TODAY MY BODY THANKED ME FOR ____________

____

____

evening wind-down

3 THINGS I'M DOING TO PROMOTE A PEACEFUL NIGHT

1. ____________
2. ____________
3. ____________

SELF-CARE checklist

- ○ bubble bath
- ○ meditate
- ○ read a good book
- ○ journal
- ○ exercise
- ○ coffee / tea
- ○ yoga
- ○ be creative
- ○ dance party
- ○ sweet treat
- ○ face mask
- ○ fun purchase
- ○ nails / beauty
- ○ deep breathing
- ○ time with a pet
- ○ gratitude list
- ○ nap / rest
- ○ call a friend
- ○ spend time outside
- ○ watch something good
- ○ game / puzzle
- ○ new restaurant
- ○ light a candle
- ○ listen to music
- ○ organize / clean
- ○ unplug
- ○ make a fun plan
- ○ affirmations
- ○ complete to-do list
- ○ do a kind act
- ○ hot shower
- ○ moment of pure peace

Self-care is giving the best of you,
not what's left of you.

You can't pour from an empty cup

A little extra self-care

Plan a trip. Sometimes the planning and anticipation of a trip are just as rewarding as the trip itself. Whether you have been contemplating your dream vacation to Hawaii, a weekend in a cozy cabin, or a staycation at a hotel in your city, take a few moments to document a getaway that excites you. Write down the activities you plan to do, food you'd like to eat, and any cozy comforts along the way (maybe some spa time or finally getting to that book you've been dying to read).

DATE: ______________________ S M T W T F S

morning gratitude

1. ______________________

2. ______________________

3. ______________________

a little beauty sleep

SLEEP DURATION — SLEPT FROM ______ to ______ TOTAL SLEEP TIME ______ hrs ______ min

SLEEP QUALITY — ☐ SOUND ☐ RESTLESS ☐ FREQUENT INTERRUPTIONS

WHAT WOKE ME — ☐ ALARM ☐ NATURALLY ☐ NOISE

HOW I FELT UPON WAKING — ☐ ENERGIZED ☐ REFRESHED ☐ TIRED ☐ GROGGY

an apple a day

NOURISHED MY BODY WITH ______________________

TREATED MY BODY WITH ______________________

DON'T FORGET TO *hydrate* ☐ ☐ ☐ ☐ ☐ ☐ ☐ ☐

exercise | stretching | meditation

TODAY MY BODY THANKED ME FOR ______________________

____

____

evening wind-down

3 THINGS I'M DOING TO PROMOTE A PEACEFUL NIGHT

1. ______________________

2. ______________________

3. ______________________

SELF-CARE
checklist

- ○ bubble bath
- ○ meditate
- ○ read a good book
- ○ journal
- ○ exercise
- ○ coffee / tea
- ○ yoga
- ○ be creative
- ○ dance party
- ○ sweet treat
- ○ face mask
- ○ fun purchase
- ○ nails / beauty
- ○ deep breathing
- ○ time with a pet
- ○ gratitude list
- ○ nap / rest
- ○ call a friend
- ○ spend time outside
- ○ watch something good
- ○ game / puzzle
- ○ new restaurant
- ○ light a candle
- ○ listen to music
- ○ organize / clean
- ○ unplug
- ○ make a fun plan
- ○ affirmations
- ○ complete to-do list
- ○ do a kind act
- ○ hot shower
- ○ moment of pure peace

Self-care is giving the best of you, not what's left of you.

DATE: ______________________ S M T W T F S

morning gratitude

1. ______________________

2. ______________________

3. ______________________

a little beauty sleep

SLEEP DURATION — SLEPT FROM ______ to ______ TOTAL SLEEP TIME ______ hrs ______ min

SLEEP QUALITY — ☐ SOUND ☐ RESTLESS ☐ FREQUENT INTERRUPTIONS

WHAT WOKE ME — ☐ ALARM ☐ NATURALLY ☐ NOISE

HOW I FELT UPON WAKING — ☐ ENERGIZED ☐ REFRESHED ☐ TIRED ☐ GROGGY

an apple a day

NOURISHED MY BODY WITH ______________________

TREATED MY BODY WITH ______________________

DON'T FORGET TO *hydrate* ☐ ☐ ☐ ☐ ☐ ☐ ☐ ☐

exercise | stretching | meditation

TODAY MY BODY THANKED ME FOR ______________________

____

____

evening wind-down

3 THINGS I'M DOING TO PROMOTE A PEACEFUL NIGHT

1. ______________________

2. ______________________

3. ______________________

SELF-CARE checklist

- ◯ bubble bath
- ◯ meditate
- ◯ read a good book
- ◯ journal
- ◯ exercise
- ◯ coffee / tea
- ◯ yoga
- ◯ be creative
- ◯ dance party
- ◯ sweet treat
- ◯ face mask
- ◯ fun purchase
- ◯ nails / beauty
- ◯ deep breathing
- ◯ time with a pet
- ◯ gratitude list
- ◯ nap / rest
- ◯ call a friend
- ◯ spend time outside
- ◯ watch something good
- ◯ game / puzzle
- ◯ new restaurant
- ◯ light a candle
- ◯ listen to music
- ◯ organize / clean
- ◯ unplug
- ◯ make a fun plan
- ◯ affirmations
- ◯ complete to-do list
- ◯ do a kind act
- ◯ hot shower
- ◯ moment of pure peace

Self-care is giving the best of you,
not what's left of you.

DATE: ______________________ S M T W T F S

morning gratitude

1. ______________________

2. ______________________

3. ______________________

a little beauty sleep

SLEEP DURATION SLEPT FROM ______ to ______ TOTAL SLEEP TIME ______ hrs ______ min

SLEEP QUALITY ☐ SOUND ☐ RESTLESS ☐ FREQUENT INTERRUPTIONS

WHAT WOKE ME ☐ ALARM ☐ NATURALLY ☐ NOISE

HOW I FELT UPON WAKING ☐ ENERGIZED ☐ REFRESHED ☐ TIRED ☐ GROGGY

an apple a day

NOURISHED MY BODY WITH ______________________

TREATED MY BODY WITH ______________________

DON'T FORGET TO *hydrate* ☐ ☐ ☐ ☐ ☐ ☐ ☐ ☐

exercise | stretching | meditation

TODAY MY BODY THANKED ME FOR ______________________

____

____

evening wind-down

3 THINGS I'M DOING TO PROMOTE A PEACEFUL NIGHT

1. ______________________

2. ______________________

3. ______________________

SELF-CARE
checklist

- ○ bubble bath
- ○ meditate
- ○ read a good book
- ○ journal
- ○ exercise
- ○ coffee / tea
- ○ yoga
- ○ be creative
- ○ dance party
- ○ sweet treat
- ○ face mask
- ○ fun purchase
- ○ nails / beauty
- ○ deep breathing
- ○ time with a pet
- ○ gratitude list
- ○ nap / rest
- ○ call a friend
- ○ spend time outside
- ○ watch something good
- ○ game / puzzle
- ○ new restaurant
- ○ light a candle
- ○ listen to music
- ○ organize / clean
- ○ unplug
- ○ make a fun plan
- ○ affirmations
- ○ complete to-do list
- ○ do a kind act
- ○ hot shower
- ○ moment of pure peace

Self-care is giving the best of you,
not what's left of you.

DATE: ______________________ S M T W T F S

morning gratitude

1. ______________________
2. ______________________
3. ______________________

a little beauty sleep

SLEEP DURATION — SLEPT FROM ________ to ________ TOTAL SLEEP TIME ________ hrs ________ min

SLEEP QUALITY — ☐ SOUND ☐ RESTLESS ☐ FREQUENT INTERRUPTIONS

WHAT WOKE ME — ☐ ALARM ☐ NATURALLY ☐ NOISE

HOW I FELT UPON WAKING — ☐ ENERGIZED ☐ REFRESHED ☐ TIRED ☐ GROGGY

an apple a day

NOURISHED MY BODY WITH ______________________

TREATED MY BODY WITH ______________________

DON'T FORGET TO *hydrate* ☐ ☐ ☐ ☐ ☐ ☐ ☐ ☐

exercise | stretching | meditation

TODAY MY BODY THANKED ME FOR ______________________

____

____

evening wind-down

3 THINGS I'M DOING TO PROMOTE A PEACEFUL NIGHT

1. ______________________
2. ______________________
3. ______________________

SELF-CARE checklist

- ○ bubble bath
- ○ meditate
- ○ read a good book
- ○ journal
- ○ exercise
- ○ coffee / tea
- ○ yoga
- ○ be creative
- ○ dance party
- ○ sweet treat
- ○ face mask
- ○ fun purchase
- ○ nails / beauty
- ○ deep breathing
- ○ time with a pet
- ○ gratitude list
- ○ nap / rest
- ○ call a friend
- ○ spend time outside
- ○ watch something good
- ○ game / puzzle
- ○ new restaurant
- ○ light a candle
- ○ listen to music
- ○ organize / clean
- ○ unplug
- ○ make a fun plan
- ○ affirmations
- ○ complete to-do list
- ○ do a kind act
- ○ hot shower
- ○ moment of pure peace

Self-care is giving the best of you,
not what's left of you.

DATE: ______________________ S M T W T F S

morning gratitude

1. ______________________

2. ______________________

3. ______________________

a little beauty sleep

SLEEP DURATION — SLEPT FROM ______ to ______ TOTAL SLEEP TIME ______ hrs ______ min

SLEEP QUALITY — ☐ SOUND ☐ RESTLESS ☐ FREQUENT INTERRUPTIONS

WHAT WOKE ME — ☐ ALARM ☐ NATURALLY ☐ NOISE

HOW I FELT UPON WAKING — ☐ ENERGIZED ☐ REFRESHED ☐ TIRED ☐ GROGGY

an apple a day

NOURISHED MY BODY WITH ______________________

TREATED MY BODY WITH ______________________

DON'T FORGET TO *hydrate* ☐ ☐ ☐ ☐ ☐ ☐ ☐ ☐

exercise | stretching | meditation

TODAY MY BODY THANKED ME FOR ______________________

____

____

evening wind-down

3 THINGS I'M DOING TO PROMOTE A PEACEFUL NIGHT

1. ______________________

2. ______________________

3. ______________________

SELF-CARE checklist

- bubble bath
- meditate
- read a good book
- journal
- exercise
- coffee / tea
- yoga
- be creative
- dance party
- sweet treat
- face mask
- fun purchase
- nails / beauty
- deep breathing
- time with a pet
- gratitude list
- nap / rest
- call a friend
- spend time outside
- watch something good
- game / puzzle
- new restaurant
- light a candle
- listen to music
- organize / clean
- unplug
- make a fun plan
- affirmations
- complete to-do list
- do a kind act
- hot shower
- moment of pure peace

Self-care is giving the best of you, not what's left of you.

*Dear Self,
I'm going to make
you proud*

A little extra self-care

As you go throughout your day, take note of at least 25 different things you are grateful for and write them down as you go. Forcing yourself to come up with a list this long will help you focus on all of the little things you have to be grateful for. It can be as small as getting a perfectly ripe avocado, choosing to wear your coziest sweater, or getting a text from a friend or family member. Gratitude work is a staple of mental and emotional self-care.

DATE: ______________ S M T W T F S

morning gratitude

1. ______________
2. ______________
3. ______________

a little beauty sleep

SLEEP DURATION — SLEPT FROM ______ to ______ TOTAL SLEEP TIME ______ hrs ______ min

SLEEP QUALITY — ☐ SOUND ☐ RESTLESS ☐ FREQUENT INTERRUPTIONS

WHAT WOKE ME — ☐ ALARM ☐ NATURALLY ☐ NOISE

HOW I FELT UPON WAKING — ☐ ENERGIZED ☐ REFRESHED ☐ TIRED ☐ GROGGY

an apple a day

NOURISHED MY BODY WITH ______________

TREATED MY BODY WITH ______________

DON'T FORGET TO *hydrate* ☐ ☐ ☐ ☐ ☐ ☐ ☐ ☐

exercise | stretching | meditation

TODAY MY BODY THANKED ME FOR ______________

____

____

evening wind-down

3 THINGS I'M DOING TO PROMOTE A PEACEFUL NIGHT

1. ______________
2. ______________
3. ______________

SELF-CARE checklist

- ○ bubble bath
- ○ meditate
- ○ read a good book
- ○ journal
- ○ exercise
- ○ coffee / tea
- ○ yoga
- ○ be creative
- ○ dance party
- ○ sweet treat
- ○ face mask
- ○ fun purchase
- ○ nails / beauty
- ○ deep breathing
- ○ time with a pet
- ○ gratitude list
- ○ nap / rest
- ○ call a friend
- ○ spend time outside
- ○ watch something good
- ○ game / puzzle
- ○ new restaurant
- ○ light a candle
- ○ listen to music
- ○ organize / clean
- ○ unplug
- ○ make a fun plan
- ○ affirmations
- ○ complete to-do list
- ○ do a kind act
- ○ hot shower
- ○ moment of pure peace

Self-care is giving the best of you,
not what's left of you.

DATE: ______________________ S M T W T F S

morning gratitude

1. ______________________

2. ______________________

3. ______________________

a little beauty sleep

SLEEP DURATION SLEPT FROM ______ to ______ TOTAL SLEEP TIME ______ hrs ______ min

SLEEP QUALITY ☐ SOUND ☐ RESTLESS ☐ FREQUENT INTERRUPTIONS

WHAT WOKE ME ☐ ALARM ☐ NATURALLY ☐ NOISE

HOW I FELT UPON WAKING ☐ ENERGIZED ☐ REFRESHED ☐ TIRED ☐ GROGGY

an apple a day

NOURISHED MY BODY WITH ______________________

TREATED MY BODY WITH ______________________

DON'T FORGET TO *hydrate*

exercise | stretching | meditation

TODAY MY BODY THANKED ME FOR ______________________

evening wind-down

3 THINGS I'M DOING TO PROMOTE A PEACEFUL NIGHT

1. ______________________

2. ______________________

3. ______________________

SELF-CARE checklist

- ◯ bubble bath
- ◯ meditate
- ◯ read a good book
- ◯ journal
- ◯ exercise
- ◯ coffee / tea
- ◯ yoga
- ◯ be creative
- ◯ dance party
- ◯ sweet treat
- ◯ face mask
- ◯ fun purchase
- ◯ nails / beauty
- ◯ deep breathing
- ◯ time with a pet
- ◯ gratitude list
- ◯ nap / rest
- ◯ call a friend
- ◯ spend time outside
- ◯ watch something good
- ◯ game / puzzle
- ◯ new restaurant
- ◯ light a candle
- ◯ listen to music
- ◯ organize / clean
- ◯ unplug
- ◯ make a fun plan
- ◯ affirmations
- ◯ complete to-do list
- ◯ do a kind act
- ◯ hot shower
- ◯ moment of pure peace

Self-care is giving the best of you,
not what's left of you.

DATE: ______________________ S M T W T F S

morning gratitude

1. ______________________

2. ______________________

3. ______________________

a little beauty sleep

SLEEP DURATION SLEPT FROM ________ to ________ TOTAL SLEEP TIME ________ hrs ________ min

SLEEP QUALITY ☐ SOUND ☐ RESTLESS ☐ FREQUENT INTERRUPTIONS

WHAT WOKE ME ☐ ALARM ☐ NATURALLY ☐ NOISE

HOW I FELT UPON WAKING ☐ ENERGIZED ☐ REFRESHED ☐ TIRED ☐ GROGGY

an apple a day

NOURISHED MY BODY WITH ______________________

TREATED MY BODY WITH ______________________

DON'T FORGET TO *hydrate*

exercise | stretching | meditation

TODAY MY BODY THANKED ME FOR ______________________

____

____

evening wind-down

3 THINGS I'M DOING TO PROMOTE A PEACEFUL NIGHT

1. ______________________

2. ______________________

3. ______________________

SELF-CARE checklist

- ○ bubble bath
- ○ meditate
- ○ read a good book
- ○ journal
- ○ exercise
- ○ coffee / tea
- ○ yoga
- ○ be creative
- ○ dance party
- ○ sweet treat
- ○ face mask
- ○ fun purchase
- ○ nails / beauty
- ○ deep breathing
- ○ time with a pet
- ○ gratitude list
- ○ nap / rest
- ○ call a friend
- ○ spend time outside
- ○ watch something good
- ○ game / puzzle
- ○ new restaurant
- ○ light a candle
- ○ listen to music
- ○ organize / clean
- ○ unplug
- ○ make a fun plan
- ○ affirmations
- ○ complete to-do list
- ○ do a kind act
- ○ hot shower
- ○ moment of pure peace

Self-care is giving the best of you,
not what's left of you.

DATE: ____________________ S M T W T F S

morning gratitude

1. ____________________

2. ____________________

3. ____________________

a little beauty sleep

SLEEP DURATION — SLEPT FROM ______ to ______ TOTAL SLEEP TIME ______ hrs ______ min

SLEEP QUALITY — ☐ SOUND ☐ RESTLESS ☐ FREQUENT INTERRUPTIONS

WHAT WOKE ME — ☐ ALARM ☐ NATURALLY ☐ NOISE

HOW I FELT UPON WAKING — ☐ ENERGIZED ☐ REFRESHED ☐ TIRED ☐ GROGGY

an apple a day

NOURISHED MY BODY WITH ____________________

TREATED MY BODY WITH ____________________

DON'T FORGET TO *hydrate* ☐ ☐ ☐ ☐ ☐ ☐ ☐ ☐

exercise | stretching | meditation

TODAY MY BODY THANKED ME FOR ____________________

____

____

evening wind-down

3 THINGS I'M DOING TO PROMOTE A PEACEFUL NIGHT

1. ____________________

2. ____________________

3. ____________________

SELF-CARE checklist

- bubble bath
- meditate
- read a good book
- journal
- exercise
- coffee / tea
- yoga
- be creative
- dance party
- sweet treat
- face mask
- fun purchase
- nails / beauty
- deep breathing
- time with a pet
- gratitude list
- nap / rest
- call a friend
- spend time outside
- watch something good
- game / puzzle
- new restaurant
- light a candle
- listen to music
- organize / clean
- unplug
- make a fun plan
- affirmations
- complete to-do list
- do a kind act
- hot shower
- moment of pure peace

Self-care is giving the best of you, not what's left of you.

DATE: ______________________ S M T W T F S

morning gratitude

1. ______________________

2. ______________________

3. ______________________

a little beauty sleep

SLEEP DURATION — SLEPT FROM ________ to ________ TOTAL SLEEP TIME ________ hrs ________ min

SLEEP QUALITY — ☐ SOUND ☐ RESTLESS ☐ FREQUENT INTERRUPTIONS

WHAT WOKE ME — ☐ ALARM ☐ NATURALLY ☐ NOISE

HOW I FELT UPON WAKING — ☐ ENERGIZED ☐ REFRESHED ☐ TIRED ☐ GROGGY

an apple a day

NOURISHED MY BODY WITH ______________________

TREATED MY BODY WITH ______________________

DON'T FORGET TO *hydrate* ☐ ☐ ☐ ☐ ☐ ☐ ☐ ☐

exercise | stretching | meditation

TODAY MY BODY THANKED ME FOR ______________________

____

____

evening wind-down

3 THINGS I'M DOING TO PROMOTE A PEACEFUL NIGHT

1. ______________________

2. ______________________

3. ______________________

SELF-CARE checklist

- ◯ bubble bath
- ◯ meditate
- ◯ read a good book
- ◯ journal
- ◯ exercise
- ◯ coffee / tea
- ◯ yoga
- ◯ be creative
- ◯ dance party
- ◯ sweet treat
- ◯ face mask
- ◯ fun purchase
- ◯ nails / beauty
- ◯ deep breathing
- ◯ time with a pet
- ◯ gratitude list
- ◯ nap / rest
- ◯ call a friend
- ◯ spend time outside
- ◯ watch something good
- ◯ game / puzzle
- ◯ new restaurant
- ◯ light a candle
- ◯ listen to music
- ◯ organize / clean
- ◯ unplug
- ◯ make a fun plan
- ◯ affirmations
- ◯ complete to-do list
- ◯ do a kind act
- ◯ hot shower
- ◯ moment of pure peace

Self-care is giving the best of you,
not what's left of you.

Take care of yourself like you're someone you love

A little extra self-care

Mentally visualizing our "happy place" can be a great calming activity. Below, take a few minutes to write down your dream happy place that you can mentally retreat to next time you are anxious or overwhelmed. Maybe you are on a hammock in an overwater bungalow in Bora Bora with the sounds of the waves crashing below you. Or maybe you are reading a book by a babbling stream in a lush forest.

DATE: ______________________ S M T W T F S

morning gratitude

1. ______________________
2. ______________________
3. ______________________

a little beauty sleep

SLEEP DURATION — SLEPT FROM ________ to ________ TOTAL SLEEP TIME ________ hrs ________ min

SLEEP QUALITY — ☐ SOUND ☐ RESTLESS ☐ FREQUENT INTERRUPTIONS

WHAT WOKE ME — ☐ ALARM ☐ NATURALLY ☐ NOISE

HOW I FELT UPON WAKING — ☐ ENERGIZED ☐ REFRESHED ☐ TIRED ☐ GROGGY

an apple a day

NOURISHED MY BODY WITH ______________________

TREATED MY BODY WITH ______________________

DON'T FORGET TO *hydrate* ☐ ☐ ☐ ☐ ☐ ☐ ☐ ☐

exercise | stretching | meditation

TODAY MY BODY THANKED ME FOR ______________________

____

____

evening wind-down

3 THINGS I'M DOING TO PROMOTE A PEACEFUL NIGHT

1. ______________________
2. ______________________
3. ______________________

SELF-CARE checklist

- ◯ bubble bath
- ◯ meditate
- ◯ read a good book
- ◯ journal
- ◯ exercise
- ◯ coffee / tea
- ◯ yoga
- ◯ be creative
- ◯ dance party
- ◯ sweet treat
- ◯ face mask
- ◯ fun purchase
- ◯ nails / beauty
- ◯ deep breathing
- ◯ time with a pet
- ◯ gratitude list
- ◯ nap / rest
- ◯ call a friend
- ◯ spend time outside
- ◯ watch something good
- ◯ game / puzzle
- ◯ new restaurant
- ◯ light a candle
- ◯ listen to music
- ◯ organize / clean
- ◯ unplug
- ◯ make a fun plan
- ◯ affirmations
- ◯ complete to-do list
- ◯ do a kind act
- ◯ hot shower
- ◯ moment of pure peace

Self-care is giving the best of you,
not what's left of you.

DATE: ______________________ S M T W T F S

morning gratitude

1. ______________________
2. ______________________
3. ______________________

a little beauty sleep

SLEEP DURATION — SLEPT FROM ______ to ______ TOTAL SLEEP TIME ______ hrs ______ min

SLEEP QUALITY — ☐ SOUND ☐ RESTLESS ☐ FREQUENT INTERRUPTIONS

WHAT WOKE ME — ☐ ALARM ☐ NATURALLY ☐ NOISE

HOW I FELT UPON WAKING — ☐ ENERGIZED ☐ REFRESHED ☐ TIRED ☐ GROGGY

an apple a day

NOURISHED MY BODY WITH ______________________

TREATED MY BODY WITH ______________________

DON'T FORGET TO *hydrate* ☐ ☐ ☐ ☐ ☐ ☐ ☐ ☐

exercise | stretching | meditation

TODAY MY BODY THANKED ME FOR ______________________

____

____

evening wind-down

3 THINGS I'M DOING TO PROMOTE A PEACEFUL NIGHT

1. ______________________
2. ______________________
3. ______________________

SELF-CARE
checklist

- ○ bubble bath
- ○ meditate
- ○ read a good book
- ○ journal
- ○ exercise
- ○ coffee / tea
- ○ yoga
- ○ be creative
- ○ dance party
- ○ sweet treat
- ○ face mask
- ○ fun purchase
- ○ nails / beauty
- ○ deep breathing
- ○ time with a pet
- ○ gratitude list
- ○ nap / rest
- ○ call a friend
- ○ spend time outside
- ○ watch something good
- ○ game / puzzle
- ○ new restaurant
- ○ light a candle
- ○ listen to music
- ○ organize / clean
- ○ unplug
- ○ make a fun plan
- ○ affirmations
- ○ complete to-do list
- ○ do a kind act
- ○ hot shower
- ○ moment of pure peace

Self-care is giving the best of you,
not what's left of you.

DATE: ______________________ S M T W T F S

morning gratitude

1. ____________________
2. ____________________
3. ____________________

a little beauty sleep

SLEEP DURATION — SLEPT FROM ______ to ______ TOTAL SLEEP TIME ______ hrs ______ min

SLEEP QUALITY — ☐ SOUND ☐ RESTLESS ☐ FREQUENT INTERRUPTIONS

WHAT WOKE ME — ☐ ALARM ☐ NATURALLY ☐ NOISE

HOW I FELT UPON WAKING — ☐ ENERGIZED ☐ REFRESHED ☐ TIRED ☐ GROGGY

an apple a day

NOURISHED MY BODY WITH ____________________

TREATED MY BODY WITH ____________________

DON'T FORGET TO *hydrate* ☐ ☐ ☐ ☐ ☐ ☐ ☐ ☐

exercise | stretching | meditation

TODAY MY BODY THANKED ME FOR ____________________

____

____

evening wind-down

3 THINGS I'M DOING TO PROMOTE A PEACEFUL NIGHT

1. ____________________
2. ____________________
3. ____________________

SELF-CARE
checklist

- ◯ bubble bath
- ◯ meditate
- ◯ read a good book
- ◯ journal
- ◯ exercise
- ◯ coffee / tea
- ◯ yoga
- ◯ be creative
- ◯ dance party
- ◯ sweet treat
- ◯ face mask
- ◯ fun purchase
- ◯ nails / beauty
- ◯ deep breathing
- ◯ time with a pet
- ◯ gratitude list
- ◯ nap / rest
- ◯ call a friend
- ◯ spend time outside
- ◯ watch something good
- ◯ game / puzzle
- ◯ new restaurant
- ◯ light a candle
- ◯ listen to music
- ◯ organize / clean
- ◯ unplug
- ◯ make a fun plan
- ◯ affirmations
- ◯ complete to-do list
- ◯ do a kind act
- ◯ hot shower
- ◯ moment of pure peace

Self-care is giving the best of you,
not what's left of you.

DATE: ______________________ S M T W T F S

morning gratitude

1. ______________________

2. ______________________

3. ______________________

a little beauty sleep

SLEEP DURATION — SLEPT FROM ________ to ________ TOTAL SLEEP TIME ________ hrs ________ min

SLEEP QUALITY — ☐ SOUND ☐ RESTLESS ☐ FREQUENT INTERRUPTIONS

WHAT WOKE ME — ☐ ALARM ☐ NATURALLY ☐ NOISE

HOW I FELT UPON WAKING — ☐ ENERGIZED ☐ REFRESHED ☐ TIRED ☐ GROGGY

an apple a day

NOURISHED MY BODY WITH ______________________

TREATED MY BODY WITH ______________________

DON'T FORGET TO *hydrate* ☐ ☐ ☐ ☐ ☐ ☐ ☐ ☐

exercise | stretching | meditation

TODAY MY BODY THANKED ME FOR ______________________

____

____

evening wind-down

3 THINGS I'M DOING TO PROMOTE A PEACEFUL NIGHT

1. ______________________

2. ______________________

3. ______________________

SELF-CARE checklist

- ○ bubble bath
- ○ meditate
- ○ read a good book
- ○ journal
- ○ exercise
- ○ coffee / tea
- ○ yoga
- ○ be creative
- ○ dance party
- ○ sweet treat
- ○ face mask
- ○ fun purchase
- ○ nails / beauty
- ○ deep breathing
- ○ time with a pet
- ○ gratitude list
- ○ nap / rest
- ○ call a friend
- ○ spend time outside
- ○ watch something good
- ○ game / puzzle
- ○ new restaurant
- ○ light a candle
- ○ listen to music
- ○ organize / clean
- ○ unplug
- ○ make a fun plan
- ○ affirmations
- ○ complete to-do list
- ○ do a kind act
- ○ hot shower
- ○ moment of pure peace

Self-care is giving the best of you,
not what's left of you.

DATE: ______________________ S M T W T F S

morning gratitude

1. ______________________
2. ______________________
3. ______________________

a little beauty sleep

SLEEP DURATION — SLEPT FROM ________ to ________ TOTAL SLEEP TIME ________ hrs ________ min

SLEEP QUALITY — ☐ SOUND ☐ RESTLESS ☐ FREQUENT INTERRUPTIONS

WHAT WOKE ME — ☐ ALARM ☐ NATURALLY ☐ NOISE

HOW I FELT UPON WAKING — ☐ ENERGIZED ☐ REFRESHED ☐ TIRED ☐ GROGGY

an apple a day

NOURISHED MY BODY WITH ______________________

TREATED MY BODY WITH ______________________

DON'T FORGET TO *hydrate* ☐ ☐ ☐ ☐ ☐ ☐ ☐ ☐

exercise | stretching | meditation

TODAY MY BODY THANKED ME FOR ______________________

____

____

evening wind-down

3 THINGS I'M DOING TO PROMOTE A PEACEFUL NIGHT

1. ______________________
2. ______________________
3. ______________________

SELF-CARE checklist

- ○ bubble bath
- ○ meditate
- ○ read a good book
- ○ journal
- ○ exercise
- ○ coffee / tea
- ○ yoga
- ○ be creative
- ○ dance party
- ○ sweet treat
- ○ face mask
- ○ fun purchase
- ○ nails / beauty
- ○ deep breathing
- ○ time with a pet
- ○ gratitude list
- ○ nap / rest
- ○ call a friend
- ○ spend time outside
- ○ watch something good
- ○ game / puzzle
- ○ new restaurant
- ○ light a candle
- ○ listen to music
- ○ organize / clean
- ○ unplug
- ○ make a fun plan
- ○ affirmations
- ○ complete to-do list
- ○ do a kind act
- ○ hot shower
- ○ moment of pure peace

Self-care is giving the best of you,
not what's left of you.

Put yourself at the top of your To-Do list

A little extra self-care

Nature is healing and spending time outdoors can be the best form of self-care. Jot down a few ways you can incorporate some outdoor time into your week. Yoga in the park, a walk in your neighborhood, or a quick and easy picnic are all great ways to get some fresh air and vitamin D.

DATE: ____________________ S M T W T F S

morning gratitude

1. ____________________
2. ____________________
3. ____________________

a little beauty sleep

SLEEP DURATION SLEPT FROM ______ to ______ TOTAL SLEEP TIME ______ hrs ______ min

SLEEP QUALITY ☐ SOUND ☐ RESTLESS ☐ FREQUENT INTERRUPTIONS

WHAT WOKE ME ☐ ALARM ☐ NATURALLY ☐ NOISE

HOW I FELT UPON WAKING ☐ ENERGIZED ☐ REFRESHED ☐ TIRED ☐ GROGGY

an apple a day

NOURISHED MY BODY WITH ____________________

TREATED MY BODY WITH ____________________

DON'T FORGET TO *hydrate* ☐ ☐ ☐ ☐ ☐ ☐ ☐ ☐

exercise | stretching | meditation

TODAY MY BODY THANKED ME FOR ____________________

____

____

evening wind-down

3 THINGS I'M DOING TO PROMOTE A PEACEFUL NIGHT

1. ____________________
2. ____________________
3. ____________________

SELF-CARE checklist

- ◯ bubble bath
- ◯ meditate
- ◯ read a good book
- ◯ journal
- ◯ exercise
- ◯ coffee / tea
- ◯ yoga
- ◯ be creative
- ◯ dance party
- ◯ sweet treat
- ◯ face mask
- ◯ fun purchase
- ◯ nails / beauty
- ◯ deep breathing
- ◯ time with a pet
- ◯ gratitude list
- ◯ nap / rest
- ◯ call a friend
- ◯ spend time outside
- ◯ watch something good
- ◯ game / puzzle
- ◯ new restaurant
- ◯ light a candle
- ◯ listen to music
- ◯ organize / clean
- ◯ unplug
- ◯ make a fun plan
- ◯ affirmations
- ◯ complete to-do list
- ◯ do a kind act
- ◯ hot shower
- ◯ moment of pure peace

Self-care is giving the best of you,
not what's left of you.

DATE: ______________________ S M T W T F S

morning gratitude

1. ______________________

2. ______________________

3. ______________________

a little beauty sleep

SLEEP DURATION — SLEPT FROM ______ to ______ TOTAL SLEEP TIME ______ hrs ______ min

SLEEP QUALITY — ☐ SOUND ☐ RESTLESS ☐ FREQUENT INTERRUPTIONS

WHAT WOKE ME — ☐ ALARM ☐ NATURALLY ☐ NOISE

HOW I FELT UPON WAKING — ☐ ENERGIZED ☐ REFRESHED ☐ TIRED ☐ GROGGY

an apple a day

NOURISHED MY BODY WITH ______________________

TREATED MY BODY WITH ______________________

DON'T FORGET TO *hydrate* ☐ ☐ ☐ ☐ ☐ ☐ ☐ ☐

exercise | stretching | meditation

TODAY MY BODY THANKED ME FOR ______________________

____

____

evening wind-down

3 THINGS I'M DOING TO PROMOTE A PEACEFUL NIGHT

1. ______________________

2. ______________________

3. ______________________

SELF-CARE
checklist

- bubble bath
- meditate
- read a good book
- journal
- exercise
- coffee / tea
- yoga
- be creative
- dance party
- sweet treat
- face mask
- fun purchase
- nails / beauty
- deep breathing
- time with a pet
- gratitude list
- nap / rest
- call a friend
- spend time outside
- watch something good
- game / puzzle
- new restaurant
- light a candle
- listen to music
- organize / clean
- unplug
- make a fun plan
- affirmations
- complete to-do list
- do a kind act
- hot shower
- moment of pure peace

Self-care is giving the best of you,
not what's left of you.

DATE: ____________________ S M T W T F S

morning gratitude

1. ____________________
2. ____________________
3. ____________________

a little beauty sleep

SLEEP DURATION — SLEPT FROM ______ to ______ TOTAL SLEEP TIME ______ hrs ______ min

SLEEP QUALITY — ☐ SOUND ☐ RESTLESS ☐ FREQUENT INTERRUPTIONS

WHAT WOKE ME — ☐ ALARM ☐ NATURALLY ☐ NOISE

HOW I FELT UPON WAKING — ☐ ENERGIZED ☐ REFRESHED ☐ TIRED ☐ GROGGY

an apple a day

NOURISHED MY BODY WITH ____________________

TREATED MY BODY WITH ____________________

DON'T FORGET TO *hydrate* ☐ ☐ ☐ ☐ ☐ ☐ ☐ ☐

exercise | stretching | meditation

TODAY MY BODY THANKED ME FOR ____________________

____

____

evening wind-down

3 THINGS I'M DOING TO PROMOTE A PEACEFUL NIGHT

1. ____________________
2. ____________________
3. ____________________

SELF-CARE checklist

- ◯ bubble bath
- ◯ meditate
- ◯ read a good book
- ◯ journal
- ◯ exercise
- ◯ coffee / tea
- ◯ yoga
- ◯ be creative
- ◯ dance party
- ◯ sweet treat
- ◯ face mask
- ◯ fun purchase
- ◯ nails / beauty
- ◯ deep breathing
- ◯ time with a pet
- ◯ gratitude list
- ◯ nap / rest
- ◯ call a friend
- ◯ spend time outside
- ◯ watch something good
- ◯ game / puzzle
- ◯ new restaurant
- ◯ light a candle
- ◯ listen to music
- ◯ organize / clean
- ◯ unplug
- ◯ make a fun plan
- ◯ affirmations
- ◯ complete to-do list
- ◯ do a kind act
- ◯ hot shower
- ◯ moment of pure peace

Self-care is giving the best of you, not what's left of you.

DATE: ______________________ S M T W T F S

morning gratitude

1. ______________________

2. ______________________

3. ______________________

a little beauty sleep

SLEEP DURATION — SLEPT FROM ______ to ______ TOTAL SLEEP TIME ______ hrs ______ min

SLEEP QUALITY — ☐ SOUND ☐ RESTLESS ☐ FREQUENT INTERRUPTIONS

WHAT WOKE ME — ☐ ALARM ☐ NATURALLY ☐ NOISE

HOW I FELT UPON WAKING — ☐ ENERGIZED ☐ REFRESHED ☐ TIRED ☐ GROGGY

an apple a day

NOURISHED MY BODY WITH ______________________

TREATED MY BODY WITH ______________________

DON'T FORGET TO *hydrate* ☐ ☐ ☐ ☐ ☐ ☐ ☐ ☐

exercise | stretching | meditation

TODAY MY BODY THANKED ME FOR ______________________

____

____

evening wind-down

3 THINGS I'M DOING TO PROMOTE A PEACEFUL NIGHT

1. ______________________

2. ______________________

3. ______________________

SELF-CARE checklist

- ○ bubble bath
- ○ meditate
- ○ read a good book
- ○ journal
- ○ exercise
- ○ coffee / tea
- ○ yoga
- ○ be creative
- ○ dance party
- ○ sweet treat
- ○ face mask
- ○ fun purchase
- ○ nails / beauty
- ○ deep breathing
- ○ time with a pet
- ○ gratitude list
- ○ nap / rest
- ○ call a friend
- ○ spend time outside
- ○ watch something good
- ○ game / puzzle
- ○ new restaurant
- ○ light a candle
- ○ listen to music
- ○ organize / clean
- ○ unplug
- ○ make a fun plan
- ○ affirmations
- ○ complete to-do list
- ○ do a kind act
- ○ hot shower
- ○ moment of pure peace

Self-care is giving the best of you,
not what's left of you.

DATE: ______________________ S M T W T F S

morning gratitude

1. ______________________
2. ______________________
3. ______________________

a little beauty sleep

SLEEP DURATION — SLEPT FROM ________ to ________ TOTAL SLEEP TIME ________ hrs ________ min

SLEEP QUALITY — ☐ SOUND ☐ RESTLESS ☐ FREQUENT INTERRUPTIONS

WHAT WOKE ME — ☐ ALARM ☐ NATURALLY ☐ NOISE

HOW I FELT UPON WAKING — ☐ ENERGIZED ☐ REFRESHED ☐ TIRED ☐ GROGGY

an apple a day

NOURISHED MY BODY WITH ______________________

TREATED MY BODY WITH ______________________

DON'T FORGET TO *hydrate* ☐ ☐ ☐ ☐ ☐ ☐ ☐ ☐

exercise | stretching | meditation

TODAY MY BODY THANKED ME FOR ______________________

____

____

evening wind-down

3 THINGS I'M DOING TO PROMOTE A PEACEFUL NIGHT

1. ______________________
2. ______________________
3. ______________________

SELF-CARE checklist

- ◯ bubble bath
- ◯ meditate
- ◯ read a good book
- ◯ journal
- ◯ exercise
- ◯ coffee / tea
- ◯ yoga
- ◯ be creative
- ◯ dance party
- ◯ sweet treat
- ◯ face mask
- ◯ fun purchase
- ◯ nails / beauty
- ◯ deep breathing
- ◯ time with a pet
- ◯ gratitude list
- ◯ nap / rest
- ◯ call a friend
- ◯ spend time outside
- ◯ watch something good
- ◯ game / puzzle
- ◯ new restaurant
- ◯ light a candle
- ◯ listen to music
- ◯ organize / clean
- ◯ unplug
- ◯ make a fun plan
- ◯ affirmations
- ◯ complete to-do list
- ◯ do a kind act
- ◯ hot shower
- ◯ moment of pure peace

Self-care is giving the best of you,
not what's left of you.

Self-care is a necessity,
not a luxury

A little extra self-care

Treat yourself! Write down a fun purchase you have been eying and then make a plan to purchase that item. It can be anything that makes you happy -- a new handbag, some personalized stationery, or some fresh flowers. Make a few notes about where and when you hope to purchase the item and any saving you need to do between now and then.

DATE: ____________ S M T W T F S

morning gratitude

1. ____________
2. ____________
3. ____________

a little beauty sleep

SLEEP DURATION — SLEPT FROM ______ to ______ TOTAL SLEEP TIME ______ hrs ______ min

SLEEP QUALITY — ☐ SOUND ☐ RESTLESS ☐ FREQUENT INTERRUPTIONS

WHAT WOKE ME — ☐ ALARM ☐ NATURALLY ☐ NOISE

HOW I FELT UPON WAKING — ☐ ENERGIZED ☐ REFRESHED ☐ TIRED ☐ GROGGY

an apple a day

NOURISHED MY BODY WITH ____________

TREATED MY BODY WITH ____________

DON'T FORGET TO *hydrate* ☐ ☐ ☐ ☐ ☐ ☐ ☐ ☐

exercise | stretching | meditation

TODAY MY BODY THANKED ME FOR ____________

____

____

evening wind-down

3 THINGS I'M DOING TO PROMOTE A PEACEFUL NIGHT

1. ____________
2. ____________
3. ____________

SELF-CARE checklist

- ○ bubble bath
- ○ meditate
- ○ read a good book
- ○ journal
- ○ exercise
- ○ coffee / tea
- ○ yoga
- ○ be creative
- ○ dance party
- ○ sweet treat
- ○ face mask
- ○ fun purchase
- ○ nails / beauty
- ○ deep breathing
- ○ time with a pet
- ○ gratitude list
- ○ nap / rest
- ○ call a friend
- ○ spend time outside
- ○ watch something good
- ○ game / puzzle
- ○ new restaurant
- ○ light a candle
- ○ listen to music
- ○ organize / clean
- ○ unplug
- ○ make a fun plan
- ○ affirmations
- ○ complete to-do list
- ○ do a kind act
- ○ hot shower
- ○ moment of pure peace

Self-care is giving the best of you,
not what's left of you.

DATE: ______________________ S M T W T F S

morning gratitude

1. ______________________
2. ______________________
3. ______________________

a little beauty sleep

SLEEP DURATION — SLEPT FROM ________ to ________ TOTAL SLEEP TIME ________ hrs ________ min

SLEEP QUALITY — ☐ SOUND ☐ RESTLESS ☐ FREQUENT INTERRUPTIONS

WHAT WOKE ME — ☐ ALARM ☐ NATURALLY ☐ NOISE

HOW I FELT UPON WAKING — ☐ ENERGIZED ☐ REFRESHED ☐ TIRED ☐ GROGGY

an apple a day

NOURISHED MY BODY WITH ______________________

TREATED MY BODY WITH ______________________

DON'T FORGET TO *hydrate* ☐ ☐ ☐ ☐ ☐ ☐ ☐ ☐

exercise | stretching | meditation

TODAY MY BODY THANKED ME FOR ______________________

____

____

evening wind-down

3 THINGS I'M DOING TO PROMOTE A PEACEFUL NIGHT

1. ______________________
2. ______________________
3. ______________________

SELF-CARE

checklist

- ○ bubble bath
- ○ meditate
- ○ read a good book
- ○ journal
- ○ exercise
- ○ coffee / tea
- ○ yoga
- ○ be creative
- ○ dance party
- ○ sweet treat
- ○ face mask
- ○ fun purchase
- ○ nails / beauty
- ○ deep breathing
- ○ time with a pet
- ○ gratitude list
- ○ nap / rest
- ○ call a friend
- ○ spend time outside
- ○ watch something good
- ○ game / puzzle
- ○ new restaurant
- ○ light a candle
- ○ listen to music
- ○ organize / clean
- ○ unplug
- ○ make a fun plan
- ○ affirmations
- ○ complete to-do list
- ○ do a kind act
- ○ hot shower
- ○ moment of pure peace

Self-care is giving the best of you,
not what's left of you.

DATE: ______________________ S M T W T F S

morning gratitude

1. ______________________
2. ______________________
3. ______________________

a little beauty sleep

SLEEP DURATION — SLEPT FROM ______ to ______ TOTAL SLEEP TIME ______ hrs ______ min

SLEEP QUALITY — ☐ SOUND ☐ RESTLESS ☐ FREQUENT INTERRUPTIONS

WHAT WOKE ME — ☐ ALARM ☐ NATURALLY ☐ NOISE

HOW I FELT UPON WAKING — ☐ ENERGIZED ☐ REFRESHED ☐ TIRED ☐ GROGGY

an apple a day

NOURISHED MY BODY WITH ______________________

TREATED MY BODY WITH ______________________

DON'T FORGET TO *hydrate*

exercise | stretching | meditation

TODAY MY BODY THANKED ME FOR ______________________

____

____

evening wind-down

3 THINGS I'M DOING TO PROMOTE A PEACEFUL NIGHT

1. ______________________
2. ______________________
3. ______________________

SELF-CARE checklist

- ◯ bubble bath
- ◯ meditate
- ◯ read a good book
- ◯ journal
- ◯ exercise
- ◯ coffee / tea
- ◯ yoga
- ◯ be creative
- ◯ dance party
- ◯ sweet treat
- ◯ face mask
- ◯ fun purchase
- ◯ nails / beauty
- ◯ deep breathing
- ◯ time with a pet
- ◯ gratitude list
- ◯ nap / rest
- ◯ call a friend
- ◯ spend time outside
- ◯ watch something good
- ◯ game / puzzle
- ◯ new restaurant
- ◯ light a candle
- ◯ listen to music
- ◯ organize / clean
- ◯ unplug
- ◯ make a fun plan
- ◯ affirmations
- ◯ complete to-do list
- ◯ do a kind act
- ◯ hot shower
- ◯ moment of pure peace

Self-care is giving the best of you,
not what's left of you.

Printed in Great Britain
by Amazon

17303312R00063